BETWEEN A BIRD CAGE
AND A BIRD HOUSE

BETWEEN A BIRD CAGE
AND A BIRD HOUSE

poems

Katerina Stoykova

UNIVERSITY PRESS OF KENTUCKY

Scholarly publisher for the Commonwealth,
serving Bellarmine University, Berea College, Centre
College of Kentucky, Eastern Kentucky University,
The Filson Historical Society, Georgetown College,
Kentucky Historical Society, Kentucky State University,
Morehead State University, Murray State University,
Northern Kentucky University, Spalding University,
Transylvania University, University of Kentucky,
University of Louisville, University of Pikeville,
and Western Kentucky University.

Editorial and Sales Offices: The University Press of Kentucky
663 South Limestone Street, Lexington, Kentucky 40508-4008
www.kentuckypress.com

Cataloging-in-Publication data available from the Library of Congress

ISBN 978-0-8131-9867-5 (hardcover)
ISBN 978-0-8131-9868-2 (paperback)
ISBN 978-0-8131-9869-9 (pdf)
ISBN 978-0-8131-9870-5 (epub)

ASSOCIATION
of UNIVERSITY
PRESSES

Member of the Association
of University Presses

CONTENTS

A.

*All I'm asking for is a reason
to throw away everything.*

America, you are so big, I feel

    endless.

Not the spider,

but the web itself.

What is the difference

between a bird cage
and a bird house.

What is the evidence
of the inevitable.

What invites
the roaming mind

looking for land.
Raising the stakes

like a barricade
against reality.

Now I see danger,
now I don't give a feather.

I want to perch on your palm
and home there.

Light without her body,

the snakeskin travels anywhere
the wind wants.

Having lost the glove of home,

free to grow at last,
the body moves on.

You know how it goes—

becoming someone else
by leaving something behind.

Stained Glass Butterflies

Fourth set of windows
this year.

America, do you remember—three weeks upon landing, I sobbed
in the basement of the English Language Multicultural Institute
out of the most confused loneliness known to my being.

A computer technician named Mitch found me,
took me to the café and bought me my first chocolate chip cookie.

Everything got better from there.

So much depends
upon

the kindness of others
to make

a foreign country
yours,

white chickens
and all.

America, what do you hide
in that bag of marbles?

The ache of every immigrant
to go back?

Ah, but you know
what it's like.

Sus-toss

*Sus-toss is a word in the Hopi language to describe the disease that
people suffer when they move to live on new lands.*

Sus-toss is a disease that makes you not want the things you want.

It makes you not want to think about
the things you want to think about.

It makes you not want to talk to your friends.
It makes you not want to have any friends.

It is the disease of living in a walnut shell
and spending all your strength to keep it closed.

When you have sus-toss you don't want to get together with people.
When you have sus-toss you don't want to be alone.

When you have sus-toss you allow yourself to only feel the joy
of work. You wear your company badge as if it were a medicine bag.

Sus-toss is the disease that urges you to be busy and work
every second of every day.

Sus-toss makes you depressed on your days off.

Sus-toss causes you to fail to see the beauty in places and people.

Sus-toss is the disease that sends different parts of you
to live in different places.

It makes you want to move from place to place
even though all places seem alike.

It is the disease of not decorating your house.

It is the disease that causes you to eat only pizza.
It makes you devour cheesecake when all you want is bread.

When you have sus-toss you are afraid to be happy.
When you have sus-toss you are afraid.

When you have sus-toss you are not as beautiful as you used to be.
When you have sus-toss you are oppressed by temporariness.

You are hoping that something will change.

Sus-toss makes you pray that
a big difficulty will come your way.

It makes you compete with everyone.
It makes you leave yourself behind to breathe your own dust.

Causes you to feel as though you are living somebody else's life.
Somebody ordinary.

Somebody who wants to be important.
Somebody who wants to be somebody.

Somebody who wants to take over the world.
Somebody terrified by the thought of not being successful.

Somebody who does not want to care about anything
and is bothered by that.

Sus-toss makes you seek proof that it was all worth it.

You can see the rest of your life and predict every day until the end.

You feel as though you are sleep-living.

Sus-toss makes you dislike yourself.

It makes you hope that you will die soon.

It feels as though you've lost your mother.

It feels as though you've moved in with your father's new wife and
now you are getting used to her cooking, her favorite colors, her
clothes. You notice that she does not save the best slice of watermel-
on for you, and you need to eat quickly from the dish, along with
everybody else.

The Country Who No Longer Wanted Her Children

Don't come back, she said.

There is nothing here, she continued.

You are better off there, she insisted.

What would you do if you returned, she resisted.

Remember why you left, she threatened.

You will regret it, she knew.

Either way, she didn't say.

America, I visited
and visited
and visited.

Visit

I visit my homeland the way a snail tries
to fit back into his old shell.
Day after day I writhe inside,
counterclockwise.

The shell is rough and narrow, opens sores
on coddled parts.

But I persist, eat tarator, cry over graves,
until I conform to my old contours. Finally,
I am here.

Snail is the most beautiful Bulgarian word,
says my son, who is studying the language.
I thought it meant *love*.

Conversation

Daddy, why is your face so sad?
Because your Mommy died, baby.

Why do you visit the grave every day, Daddy?
Baby, she's there every day.

Daddy, your pillow is bitter with salt.
Is that a question, baby?

The Way I Pray to St. Catherine

In the church,
I light a candle.

I walk up to the icon,
squat an inch

so that my eyes   align with hers.

I look at her,
she looks at me,

we stay this way
until she knows

everything.

America, you made me
in your image, then prescribed
the exercise of looking in the mirror,
repeating *I love myself*
while gazing into my own eyes.

America, I love myself
being yours.

He Catches a Magic Fish

1.

He: Will you make my dreams come true?
She: Yes, yes, but you must let me go first.
He: What if all I want is to be with you?

2.

She tries to vanish, but
when it doesn't work, she's left
with the choice of trying
to make a go of it, for now
she has no other powers.
He seems happy. All he
really wants is a fish to feed
in a round aquarium by his TV.
Every day she is steeped
in the safe soup of her life.
I don't know what happened,
she thinks, and swims out
of a wrecked ship by a gaudy
treasure chest and fake seaweed
for a gulp of air, then, again, sinks.
What happened, she asks
a plastic skull with jaws

permanently sprawled
and bejeweled eyes.
What happened?

A man and a woman in a bedroom

The woman lying in bed,
the man sitting by her,
rubbing her ankles and feet.
Nobody speaks.
She thinks about her trip,
he thinks about his work.
The spouses are together
in the same room,
which is rare.
His gaze wanders.
He reads out loud
titles of self-help books
scattered across the floor.
Healing Your Aloneness;
Inner Bonding;
Do I Have to Give Up Me
to Be Loved by You?
She has shut her eyes.
In a minute he'll kiss her
goodnight and leave
for another room.
He had given her a cute
coupon for massage
of two body parts
and tonight
both were redeemed.

Once

I bit into an apple and said,
He and I will be finished
by the time this apple rots.
I kept it at my desk;
the bite marks curled
inward, the white flesh
scabbed toward its softness.
This lasted days upon days.
Then I said to myself,
I want to save this apple,
so I locked it in the fridge.
Already the apple was leaning
into its wound—headfirst
without a face
in its cold home, furrows
growing deeper.
From time to time
I'd pick up the apple
and assess.
It's okay, I'd say.
It's okay, considering.

America, you watched me change.
You gave me a hand

and a hand
and a hand.

You gave me everything
I asked for,

and I gave you
twenty years in exchange.

Honey, this is the scary truth.

The ring on your finger
does not protect you

from your heart,
despite the way at times

your heart protects you
from the ring on your finger.

More often, though,
it is what it is,

you are who you are,
and you are sorry, but

try as you might
you cannot feel

what you promised
before that immigration judge.

By now you don't know
how to wake up

even as your life force seeps
like the sap of a sliced grapevine,

even as your heart overhears
the vague noise

of some distant you
humming a different day,

while you sit here, staring
at that link in your chain.

To the Foreign Woman Who Called Her Daughter „Скотина" for Untying Her Shoes in the Post Office; Beaumont Branch, Lexington, KY, 4/18/2013

Somebody always listens.
Somebody always understands, sees, feels
what you say.

I wouldn't want to be her,
your little girl with pink sneakers
staring numbly into the floor.

I wouldn't want to be you—
a beacon of bile, arms crossed over
the chest that helped you emigrate.
Life appears to not be
what he promised. The beauty
you traded in for comfort—
half vanished; the comfort itself—
now taken for granted.

Nor your meek American husband, resigned
to this upgrade to loneliness 1.1, your
strange meals, barbed glances, loaded
silences; submitted to living in fear
of having a different opinion.

Neither the elderly female relative
with her back
to all of us, pretending
to be engrossed in the merchandise
of padded envelopes and comical postcards.

The girl walks up to her
and looks at cats with large eyes,
dancing groundhogs, thank you notes
for the fact that nobody here
speaks foreign languages.

Little girl, before it gets better,
I'm sorry to say, it will get worse.
If I could, I'd tell her „Опомнитесь,"
but she scares me too.

For what is worth, one day she will want to erase
what she just said and instead
kneel down to help and continue to teach you,
for she'll know nothing matters more
than her only daughter
being able to walk well.

Until then, it's okay to cry for the losses
and accept the love. „Любимая“
is what your mother should have said to you.
I'd tell her that I know.

I know, I'd tell her.
I'm so sorry.
I know.

Dear Numbness,

you are a funny kind of snail—
instead of in a shell, you crawl around
your own freezer. You doubt anyone
would understand. You hate your heart
frosting into a snowball, but you need
a safe space. Nobody can hurt you there,
yet you wait for it to melt.
Hard to believe
all this cold
intact
in hell.

America, here is the answer to the question

What's between me and being fine:

It's not you.

It's me.

Dear One,

it's not your fault
    once you were young
and it's not my fault
    I was hopeless
    and didn't have a dime
and it's not his fault
    he fell in love with us
and it's not your fault
    you called him Dad
and it's not my fault
    I said I do
and it's not my fault
    I ate his food
and it's not his fault
    he was good to us
and it's not your fault
    you went to school
and it's not my fault
    I let you grow
    into a father and son
and it's not his fault
    he was the only one
and it's not my fault
    I said I love you
    with a closed heart

and it's not his fault
    he never realized
and it's not your fault
    you turned into a fine young man
    because of him
and it's not my fault
    I denied myself
and it's not his fault
    he was the good guy
and it's not your fault
    you grew up and left
    me and him without us
and it's not my fault
    I feel I've lost my life
and it's not his fault
    he's happy
    with the way things are.

There once was a woman who wanted to be a better mother

than her own mother.
This was a big and important goal
and she never stopped talking about it.
To whom? To her own little girl.

She listed examples—and examples
abounded—what a great mother she
(herself) was, and how her own mother
had failed. She spoke with emotion.

With disgust. Perhaps with a bit
of admiration toward herself?
No. More like self-pity. The child
heard the following: "It's your fault,

it's your fault, it's your fault." However,
that's not what the mother was saying.
The mother wanted someone to hear
that she hadn't had the mother she'd needed.

Yet the daughter concluded: "You're bad
because you have it good." And the mother
was so busy criticizing her
own mother in front of the child

that the child, little by little, started
to take care of the mother,
to console her, to listen,
and to keep her terrifying secrets.

Both got along great. "My daughter
is my best friend!" bragged the mother
and the daughter beamed, felt
both important and praised.

And ultimately she became a better
mother for her mother. Or at least
a joyful lump of light in her heart
believed it and wanted it to be so.

America, there will be nothing left
to say,
but not yet.

Shame is a private punishment.

Miserable doesn't mean **innocent**.

By the way **it hurts** you'll know what it means.

Truth comes with its own complications.

If you can't feel anything, that **doesn't mean** it's not hurting.

There is no **beauty** in sadness. No honor in suffering. No growth in fear. No relief in hate. It's just a waste of perfectly good happiness.

I Shame, Therefore I Am

The shame is mightier than the sword

The squeaky wheel gets the shame

People who live in shame houses should not throw stones

Hope for the best but prepare for the shame

Keep your enemies close and your shame closer

There is no shame like home

Shameliness is next to godliness

Shamers can't be choosers

All good things must come to a shame

Shame is the best medicine

Patience is a shame

Don't shame your chickens before they hatch

You reap what you shame, then shame what you sow

Better shame than sorry

Honesty is the best shame

Discretion is the greater part of shame

There is no such thing as free shame

Shame is the mother of invention

Shame helps those who help themselves

No shame, no gain

Shame happens

Practice makes shame, shame makes perfect

If you want shame done right, you have to do it yourself

Wasn't it easier with less awareness?

Simpler, at least.
I don't know

why I'm doing this—
enough of an answer.

The rest—opaque,
wall-to-wall fog,

the shoulders shrugged
into *Don't ask.*

We write our way to truth,
Kathleen said. That's perhaps why

I keep on scribbling,
transmitting words.

Contrary to popular belief,
they don't talk back.

Words on the page lay quiet,
see through, dig deep,

and I have learned
which ones to keep.

America, I love doing stupid things
with you,
for you.
Thank you.

At some point you stopped

offering me your life

your home the key
quit fitting into the lock

you stopped waiting for me

to say *yes* I didn't know
I could run out of time

what do we do now

that we're still alive
at both ends of without

who will be the first

to hobble away
I hope it's me

but I don't see how

The entire day I loved someone.

When I returned home, I knew—
it wasn't you.

Wasn't me either.

Meanwhile,
love had seeped
into the cracks of the parquet floor,
between the rubber goosebumps
of the slippers.

Meanwhile,
love was left
in a cab
or on a chair,
or it retreated
into the lifeline of a glove.

We sat down for dinner.
I reached and touched your face
over two plates
of rice and tomatoes.

There were no words
but the television,
and the question

Why am I here?
pulsed in the air
while the silence continued.

It's a Great Day to Burn, the Man Said.

He meant: *It's nice outside,*
not too much wind, the dew
has lifted, and you can
light a match to your old
poems ripped from journals
because you don't want anyone
to read them in case you decide
to die and actually go through with it.
That last bit I added in my head,
but he suspected as much.
This is why he locked his gun
and hid the key. The bullets lived
in a ceramic bowl in the bedroom.
One could confuse them with hard candy.
The revolver used to lie
by his head. He said he needed it
to feel safe, since he worked with inmates,
but I think he liked knowing that
at any moment he could kill someone.
I made up that last part. He wanted
to keep me alive. I was the one slipping
in and out of the sweet urge to die.
Yes, sweet. I meant that.

Wanna come burn with me? The man asked
his little dog, and she followed him
to the backyard.

Some Catastrophes Approach Slowly.

Everyone can see them. Even you. Close your eyes, still see them. Saying no to a catastrophe becomes harder in proportion to the time you've spent staring at it, multiplied by the time you've spent refusing to think about it. What is there to consider? All is clear. The catastrophe wants you to be there, waiting, as if on a romantic date. There must be something that pulls you toward it because, even though your heart is gripped in horror, you cannot look away. You wonder what the attraction is but prefer to be surprised by the pain and the ruin you suspect will follow. The regret and the shame, fluttering like a cape close behind. And then the damn footprints of the long walk of rebuilding your life, the Bible-thick litany of losses. The jump-starts, the false-starts, the near-deaths. The hobbling ahead.

America, it's complicated.
America, please,
don't be mad. There are places
in me so distant
even you can't expand.

Eighth Floor Balcony Ghazal

If I catch you smoking
I'll throw you off the balcony.

If something happens to you
I'll jump off the balcony.

Dad stopped hitting me: Go ahead, he laughed, scream for help.
Then opened the door to the balcony.

To free space in the kitchen,
we moved the stove to the balcony.

Dad got mad and started
dragging Mom toward the balcony.

You could see the sun rise
out of the Black Sea from the balcony.

When the guests for Mom's funeral arrived,
Dad hid, smoking on the balcony.

I've been faking all my orgasms,
I confessed to my first ex-husband on the balcony.

I stared out for a month, waiting for my pen pal to arrive,
as I was scrubbing the windows on the balcony.

Your marriage will last at most three years,
Dad told me on the balcony.

When I was leaving for America, I looked up from the cab and saw
my best friend waving from the balcony.

I'm ready to let go of everything that happened
except the balcony.

Katerina, there is no heaven or hell,
there is just this balcony.

So, You Miss Your Depression.
So, You Cherish Your Loneliness.

Oh, how good it feels
to be back in touch
with the autoerotic self-pity.
Ah, the one-armed swimming,
the single oar circling
away from solace.
You don't really want
to feel better, do you?
Stranded in the emotional soup
like a frog on a water lily,
what if you never write
anything better?
Anything ever?
What if you've trailed mistakes,
year after year,
in the branch tree of
bad decisions?
Potential is
as potential does,
despite how smart
you believe you are.
How far have you strayed
from your real life?

I don't know

where you came from, little feather
stuck in my shirt, but stay there,
blade first.

America, if your eyes are dry
you never loved me.

Yes, you gave,
but I sacrificed.

Better

for Toni

The time I left
my best friend behind

was a time of hope
for something better

than a best friend,

was a time of hope
for true love,

was a time of hope
for a better life, better

than a best friend,
better than her

true love, better

than a life
with my best friend, better

than holding hands
on busted streets, better

than sharing
the cheapest ice cream, better

than her lithe body spooning mine
in the hotel room by the US consulate, better

than our unconditional love
unless I find

something better.

The time I left
my best friend behind,

there were parts of me
I left her. I left her.

Darling,

for the past twenty years
I've been trying to meet you,
to gauge if you love me still,
if I love you still, and if both
were true, to steal you
from your wife.
Just last night, when
I dreamed of you again
I saw the possibilities
of life together, splendid
happiness, triumph
of forgiveness. The young
know best. And we did.
How are your children?
In my dream we played
together, the older
claimed I'm her
role model and we wore
the same color skirts.
The missus was cooking
through all this, the whole time
beaming at me while
you and I discussed
signing papers, seeing
each other again.
Darling, I know I was the one

who took off
with another. Had I not
done that and other stupid
things, we may have kept.
Like last night I waited
half an hour in one spot
on the street until
you ran up to me, dressed
in your white Navy uniform
and hugged me
with so much love,
I had to sit down.

Everybody needs a pen

to scrawl what they can tell
everyone else but
that one person.

America, what you have
I do not want.
Though you have a lot.

You'll be given
everything, twice.

Once—to lose it
in order to live

through that. The second
time is yours

to decide: everything
you've ever wanted

for everything
you've ever had.

By the end
of your life, you

will have fed
one life to another,

will have dug
one ditch to fill another,

will have traversed
one side of the map,

until you reach the tip
of its root.

One is enough, you think.
One would have been

enough, you want
to believe.

You look for proof
that others are wrong,

hard proof
you've made

better choices
when you didn't

do what you wanted
and they did.

Look at them now, and
look at you.

Whoever looks last
sees what's left.

America, if there were a rule
about being happy together,

we did what we could.

At least we better honed
the bit about gratitude.

The Body, the Collateral

1. The body

misses the body it used to wrap itself around. You cannot convince the body, *Body, don't miss that body. It had a personality incompatible with yours.* The body longs for the shape of the body in bed. Its shade in the shower. The buttons of the shirts. The body misses the body's hair, skin imperfections. The body's not rational, reasonable, just recognizes the lack. A world without a body is less of a world. The body misses the senses of the body. The body wants to cry. The body feels a slash in its chest, looks down, everything seems fine. The body doesn't know what's happening. The body is dumb, knows nothing of careless spending and credit card balances. The body wants what the body wants. The body is alone in bed. The body bears this stabbing pain, looks down, all seems well. The body slouches toward the ache. The body rejects everything. Food's overrated; nuisance—hot shower. The body wants to hold the body's hand through the night. The body is ailing without the body. The body is waiting. The body will agree to anything, just bring back the body. The body has never felt so alone. The body is inconvincible. You cannot lie to the body. Try to bait and switch with another body and the body will shut down—it wants the body, the body is what it craves, eyes open wide in the night. These are not the arms, this is not the chest, these are not the lean legs of the body it wants. The body longs to get out of bed and look for the body. To seek until it finds. The body believes it's been thumbtacked through the middle. The body remembers the pleasure and won't give it up. The body is sad. Yes, the body is sad.

2. The body

is getting used to the body. The body is warm, breathes in and out, provides heat in the night. The body holds the body's hand during sleep, and the body likes that. The body accepts the body. The body fills the space. The body feels good to the body, the more familiar it feels, the more it feels safe. The body notices how its heart unseals, and a puff of love slides towards the body. The body doesn't understand how but grows both thankful and surprised. Thus the body works. The body is getting used to the body. The body starts to imagine it can live such a life.

3. The body

adores the body. The body laughs and floats above the bed, above the streets, above its own troubles, the body drinks heat from the body, sleeps nestled into it, linked through the bodies' sex parts. The bodies do not part. *I didn't know I could be this happy,* the body marvels. The body doesn't wonder, yet senses wonder, presses itself to the body. The body glows with a glow visible to everybody. The body is different, everything is different, the body is the world, the body is the self, the body wants the body to feel good. The body cooks food and eats together with the body, side by side, legs touching. The body holds the body tight. Says, *Mine.* The body likes the thought of being somebody's. The body smiles, the body stays. The body is the body is the body. The body is real. The body understands love. The body eases into a wave of relief. Thank you, the body says.

. . . and in the morning, we saw a moth.

Fused headfirst
to the shallow tin

of a burned-out tealight.
Wings glazed with wax.

Antennae set into the wick,
and every pair of his legs

pressed into a prayer.
Done. Gone out with the light.

What a way to propagate
your cautionary tale, friend!

What a way to stay
a monument to love.

America, now I know.

You are my home
away from home.
My life
away from my life.

We Must Be Very Careful When Using the Word *Home.*

At home, at our apartments.
Two kilometers on foot
from the cemetery and
our mothers' rectangles. At home,
where it's tragic and filled
with our own existence. At home,
we can find honey, mint tea,
know everyone's secrets. At home
we suspect our neighbors.
We do not spit in the elevator. We
receive letters. We may be in love
or may not be. That doesn't matter.
We are, and love is. At home
there is an old, reddish chair, where
we wrote our first poem. At home
every object is owned by an emotion.
Time has stopped as if everything
were waiting to see us. At home—
that means we've been needed. At home—
a record number of ghosts.
One dresses our wounds,
another—a salad, a third asks about
living abroad—he also wants
to see where his happiness lies.

There is more. We only have to pull
open a drawer. We take items out,
put them back, close—
stairs of ourselves we've climbed,
for which there is no space where we live,
but we can keep them at home.

Black Stone over White Stone

After César Vallejo

I will die in Bourgas, under the pouring rain
that falls once a year
or two, whenever I can visit.
I will die on the eighth-floor balcony, at sunrise
as the sky tugs the sun's soul out
of the Black Sea shimmer.

It will be a Friday, as it is today,
because as I write these lines, I notice
how the work week ends and how
I crawl into another
pile—unfinished business.

Katerina died— during her visit.
Whoever is returning to Kentucky
isn't she, believe me. Determined
to remain unnoticed, this person mirrors
her disappearing foreign bones completely.

The only witnesses remain
the balcony, the rain,
the constant resurrections.

America, I don't know
what to do with you.

What would you do with me
if you had to do something?

I know, you'd let me be
anything.

And that's everything.

The Apple Who Wanted to Become a Pinecone

(An Interview)

Q: I can see why a pinecone would wish to be an apple, but it is less obvious why an apple would want to be a pinecone. Why do it?

A: Well . . . maybe I would like having hundreds of arms. Maybe I would enjoy letting air reach the rope of my core. Maybe I want to resemble a fish and a tree at the same time. Is that so difficult to believe?

Q: Is there anything you'd miss about being an apple?

A: No. I am tired of being sweet, round, and shiny. I no longer want to smell good. I hate being food for humans. It bugs me when they look at me and salivate. I am tired of keeping their stupid doctor away. And I am afraid of worms.

Q: How will you go about turning into a pinecone?

A: First, I'll elongate, then I'll shrink at the waist, then I'll develop scales and produce a seed for each. I'll dry up and turn brown, my favorite color.

And I will fall far, far from the tree.

A Dream

At my feet—a stack of fish scales.

One by one I pick them up
and glue them to my body.

I resemble a half-done
3D puzzle of a fish.

I think I may be a trout.

Why in the world are you doing this?
A passerby cries.

I open and close,
open and close,

open and close
my mouth.

America, would you be a part of me
but not me?

Would you let me keep whole?

I love you.
Don't let me go.

Imagine a raw egg. Още в черупката. The shell is whole. После я чупиш на две. You do that carefully so that the contents remain intact. Then you try pouring the egg into just one of its jagged cups, but now it no longer fits, so you must either leave some behind or never stop going back and forth. Така се усеща имиграцията.

Представи си сурово яйце. Still in its shell. Черупката е цяла. Then you break it in two. Правиш го внимателно, така че съдържанието да остане невредимо. После се опитваш да прелееш яйцето в само една от неговите назъбени чашки, но то вече не се побира, така че трябва или да изоставиш част от него, или да не спираш да го придвижваш напред назад. This is what it feels like to immigrate.

Creative Spurt

By now the moon has shrunk back
to a dark comma in the sky,
and I have stopped writing.

Two weeks of rubbing pen and paper
like a cicada rubs its front legs, and erupting
in some language I no longer use

for thinking. They say the tongue
you become a poet in is the one
that can never tell a lie.

If it leaves me now, who will miss it?
How could I live with it, without it?

As I'm writing this

a warbler attempts to grasp
the glass pane.
Listen, Friend.
I understand.

America, I dally
by the airplane door.
The sacred pipe you gave me
cradled inside my carry-on.
Leaving on time, the monitor says.

I hope so.

Bo from the Choctaw Nation: The tunnel in the stem of your pipe is not carved but burrowed out. The pipe maker opens a pit, small enough to fit a sumac beetle, places it there, then presses his thumb over the exit. After mere seconds the bug starts digging forward, through the core, without stopping, until it comes out the other end.

Katerina: Is there no danger that the beetle could turn back and bite your finger?

Bo: Yes, they do that sometimes, but it doesn't hurt. Plus, they quickly realize that's the only way.

What Happens to the Prophet

who returns
to the town of his birth?

What happens to the wolf
who returns
to his own blood?

What happens to the wave
who returns
to her own sea?

What happens to the wave
who stays away?

B.

*If everything is going your way,
then why are you so sad?*

Theorem: *America is the greatest country in the world.*

Proof

There once was a man who kept on falling in love
with foreign women, then learning their languages.
The process required time and effort, money
for lessons, but it was well worth it. He liked to give
this gesture to the women whom he wanted
to bring into his country, for he planned on
marrying them, as well. He owned a big-enough house
with a designated room where the bride-to-be
could live, without being too much in the way.

See, these women had no way of knowing that
as soon as they arrived and were given orientation
into the new world, his efforts would cease.
He didn't study the languages to make them feel special,
but to facilitate conversations with foreign women since
no American ones would give him the time of day.

American women have demands just for existing, he'd grumble.

What were these American women thinking,
having demands? I don't know, but the foreign ones
seemed exceedingly forgiving, eager to please for a lot less
in return. One might say they were desperate
to leave their pathetic, hopeless countries.

What would they receive in this arrangement?
Food, shelter, financial security, appearance
of a relationship. Not a lot of demands
were placed on them. They didn't have to cook or clean.
Getting a job was optional. They simply had to *be there*.
Had to exist in the house, preferably in their own room,
which they were free to leave, of course. In exchange
for all this American goodness, the women had to give up
a few things: their hopes to have children, or even
sex for that matter, save for the bimonthly
conjugal event that they had to explicitly request.
The women performed the duty of *being there*,
for he wanted somebody. And whenever that happened,

all was well.

At some point, however, the women would grow
inexplicably depressed: unable to get out of bed, staring
at some stain in the air, would stop bathing, speaking,
or leaving the house. Whenever the man noticed,
he would do his best to ignore the issue for as long as possible,
and when he no longer could,
he would put them on a plane
to go back to wherever they came from.

Clean. Easy. Final.
Not terribly expensive, either.

He did want somebody, however, so whenever one left,
he immediately got busy looking for another.
That wasn't difficult. The process resembled shopping
from a catalog. As an intelligent, self-respecting man,
he dismissed the cheap-looking girls in provocative bikinis,
went straight for the gorgeous ones with advanced degrees,
even though they would never be able to practice
upon landing in the USA. One way or another,
no shortage of foreign beauties for our man.
As I'm writing this, the future missus is packing
her suitcase with whatever she holds dear
to bring her tight little body and old-world potential
into the room she will need to fill.

Conclusion

See what your country can do for you?

He did want somebody, however, so whenever one left,
he immediately started looking for another. Years
rolled along. Technologies changed. The man aged.
The women—not so much. One of them,
from the country of B. (he only brought women from countries
that started with the letter B) seemed more resilient than the rest,
determined to not be "shipped back," as he would threaten.
She learned to drive, went to school, got skills, then jobs,
built a support system and drew strength from it.
When a few years passed, she received the citizenship
certificate and focused on her goals and priorities.
America opened to her, with all its vastness
and possibilities, and she grew to love it and think of it
as her own. Throughout all this, yes, the woman fulfilled
her one and only marital duty of _being there,_ until
one day she was done. The woman left _the man_
and lived happily ever after. _In America._

Alternate Conclusion

See what your country can do for you.

Acknowledgments and Notes

This manuscript has been developed in part with the financial support of the Kentucky Foundation for Women.

The author would like to thank the editors of the following magazines, websites, and collections where these poems first appeared:

Good River Review, inaugural issue, 2021: "A man and a woman in a bedroom," "Once"

Still: The Journal, fall 2021: "So, You Miss Your Depression. So, You Cherish Your Loneliness," "What is the difference"

30/30 Project, Tupelo Press, 2013: ". . . and in the morning, we saw a moth," "He Catches a Magic Fish" (first published as "He Catches a Gold Fish")

Diode Poetry Journal, fourteenth anniversary edition: "*It's a Great Day to Burn,* the Man Said," "To the Foreign Woman Who Called Her Daughter „Скотина" for Untying Her Shoes in the Post Office; Beaumont Branch, Lexington, KY, 4/18/2013"

The Air around the Butterfly, Fakel Express, 2009 [out of print]: "A Dream," "Sus-toss," "The Apple Who Wanted to Become a Pinecone"

The Porcupine of Mind, Broadstone Books, 2012 [out of print]: "Better," "Creative Spurt," "The Way I Pray to St. Catherine" (first published as "The Way I Used to Pray to St. Catherine"), "Visit," "What Happens to the Prophet"

Second Skin, ICU Publishing, 2019: "Conversation," "Black Stone over White Stone," "Eighth Floor Balcony Ghazal," "We Must Be Very Careful When Using the Word *Home*"

Poems & Plays, 2014: "Darling,"

How God Punishes, 2016, Broadstone Books: "By the end of your life," "You'll be given everything, twice," "You look for proof," "Bo from the Choctaw Nation"

Yearling, 2023: "The Body, the Collateral"

Lexington Poetry Month website, 2019: "I Shame, Therefore I Am,"

Bird on a Window Sill, Publishing House Signs, 2017: "Shame is a private punishment"

South 85, 2022: "Imagine a raw egg"

So much depends upon

This poem follows the structure of William Carlos Williams's famous poem "The Red Wheelbarrow."

Sus-toss

I learned word "sus-toss" from my former mentor Jeremie Leckron.

Visit

The words "snail" and "love" are „охлюв" and „любов," respectively, in Bulgarian. They do sound alike.

To the Foreign Woman Who Called Her Daughter „Скотина" for Untying Her Shoes in the Post Office; Beaumont Branch, Lexington, KY, 4/18/2013

The foreign words in this poem come from the Russian language and respectively mean "stupid cow," "come to your senses," and "beloved."

Wasn't it easier with less awareness?

The "Kathleen" mentioned in the poem is my mentor Kathleen Driskell.

The Body, the Collateral

"Says, Mine" is borrowed from a pantoum by Cecilia Woloch.

Black Stone over White Stone

This poem follows the general form and borrows several expressions from the famous poem by César Vallejo of the same name.

About the Author

Katerina Stoykova is the author of several award-winning poetry books in English and Bulgarian, as well as senior editor of Accents Publishing. Her latest book, *Second Skin* (ICU, 2018, Bulgarian), received the Vanya Konstantinova Biannual National Poetry Award as well as a grant from the European Commission's program Creative Europe for translation and publication in English. Katerina acted in the lead roles for the independent feature films *Proud Citizen* and *Fort Maria*, both directed by Thom Southerland. Her poems have been translated into German, Spanish, Bangla, Farsi, and Ukrainian, and a volume of her selected poems, translated into Arabic by acclaimed poet Khairi Hamdan, was published by Dar Al Biruni press in 2022.

Katerina immigrated to the United States in 1995 and has lived in Lexington, Kentucky, since 2004.